CIRQUE DU SOLEIL®

VAREKAI™

CIRQUE DU SOLEIL®

VAREKAI™

Written and Directed
by Dominic Champagne

Photographs by Véronique Vial

Text by Kerry Fleming

Harry N. Abrams, Inc., Publishers

Editor: Christopher Sweet
Designer: Judy Hudson, Biproduct
Production Manager: Justine Keefe

**Library of Congress Cataloging-in-
Publication Data**
Vial, Véronique.
 Cirque du Soleil : Varekai / photographs
by Véronique Vial ; text by Kerry Fleming.
       p.   cm.
ISBN 0–8109–4442–1
1. Cirque du Soleil—Pictorial works.
2. Varekai. I. Title: Varekai.
II. Fleming, Kerry. III. Title.
GV1821.C578V53 2003
791.3'09714—dc21
2002043744

Printed and bound in China

Harry N. Abrams, Inc.
100 Fifth Avenue
New York, N.Y. 10011
www.abramsbooks.com

Abrams is a subsidiary of
LA MARTINIÈRE
G R O U P E

The Characters

Icarus

Olga

The Guide

The Limping Angel

The Skywatcher

The Volcano Leapers

Le Caporal

Carmencita

Le Dandy

La Diseuse

Le Fantôme

La Petite Lune

Claudio

Mooky

Castor

Pollux

The Icarian Brothers

The Goddesses

The Gatherers

The Firemasters

The Juggler & The Lizard

Daedalus

The Muse

enter the forest

abandon your fears

everything possible happens right here

beneath your feet

creatures conspire

above

the fireflies licking higher

and in between the light and dark

a story unfolds

a graceful arc

                        what if

                        what then

The word *Varekai*™ is Romani for "wherever." And from that word, an idea: *no matter where the wind carries you, you'll always be home*. The creators started with a premise. What if Icarus hadn't fallen into the sea? What if he had fallen into a mysterious forest, inhabited by strange beings? How would his life have changed?

As *Varekai* opens, Icarus falls to earth. But with his fall comes renaissance – a chance to be born anew. Thus begins a journey of self-realization. Along the path, Icarus meets a bewildering cast of creatures and characters, some of whom oppose his bid for greatness; others guide and support him as he strives once again to reach new heights.

In many ways, *Varekai* is a celebration of our collective desire to rise above – free of our terrestrial ties. Where the myth of Icarus ends, *Varekai* begins. Welcome to the making of an angel.

In Greek mythology, Icarus was the son of Daedalus, an artisan commissioned by the King of Crete to design a prison for the Minotaur. Daedalus built the Labyrinth. Later, Daedalus helped two other prisoners – Theseus and Ariadne – escape from the Labyrinth and in doing so, betrayed the King. Daedalus and Icarus were imprisoned in a tower on an island from which there was no escape . . . or so the King thought. Daedalus fashioned two sets of wings from feathers and wax for himself and his son.

Before their flight to freedom, Daedalus gave his son a warning: *if you fly too close to the sea, your wings will become too heavy for flight; if you fly too close to the sun, the wax will melt*. Alas, young Icarus was swept up by his own excitement and pride and he forgot his father's warning. He flew too close to the sun. The wax melted, his wings came apart, and he fell to his death in the ocean near the Island of Damos. Today, those waters are still known as the Icarian sea.

For people around the world, Icarus is a symbol of youthful insouciance and arrogance, but he also represents courage and our desire to excel.

The "Grand Chapiteau" (or Big Top) – does not house a stage, but a universe . . . a world unto itself. *Varekai* begins the moment you arrive. Before you've even taken your seat, you are entranced by marmots and musicos, lizards and leapers. Creatures slither across the stage and wander among the audience. A feeling begins to grow: anything is possible here.

Celebration

The underworld groans and shakes. Gasses hiss from cracks in the earth. Winds whip frantically, lashing at the trees. There's something in the air. Something must be done. The Guide – a mystical emcee – takes his place and presides over a ritual incantation, a chaotic choreography of dancers, acrobats, and animals calling out to the heavens. All eyes are skyward. All souls are ready. The message is clear: *Send us your chosen one.*

how proud

    we stood in awe

basking in his vainglory

    our eyes trained

ever towards heaven

on the wings of pride

    he rose

at death's request

    he fell

a feather into our waiting arms

welcome home son

Incantation

The community gathers round. Bowed down. Waiting. The heavens open as our spent star, our angel, makes his fall from grace. Icarus, wings aflutter, comes to rest at our feet.

The Guide is there to receive him. A solemn greeting indeed. The Skywatcher, a birdlike creature, plucks at the wings, enacting his own mock flight as the villagers fight over the spoils. Tenderly, the Guide rolls Icarus up in a shroud and the heavens take back their own.

again

    to dance once more

again

    a chance to soar

    from fire to ashes

    ashes to dust

    release me from this death unjust

    renew my spirit

    voice my name

    grant me life

again

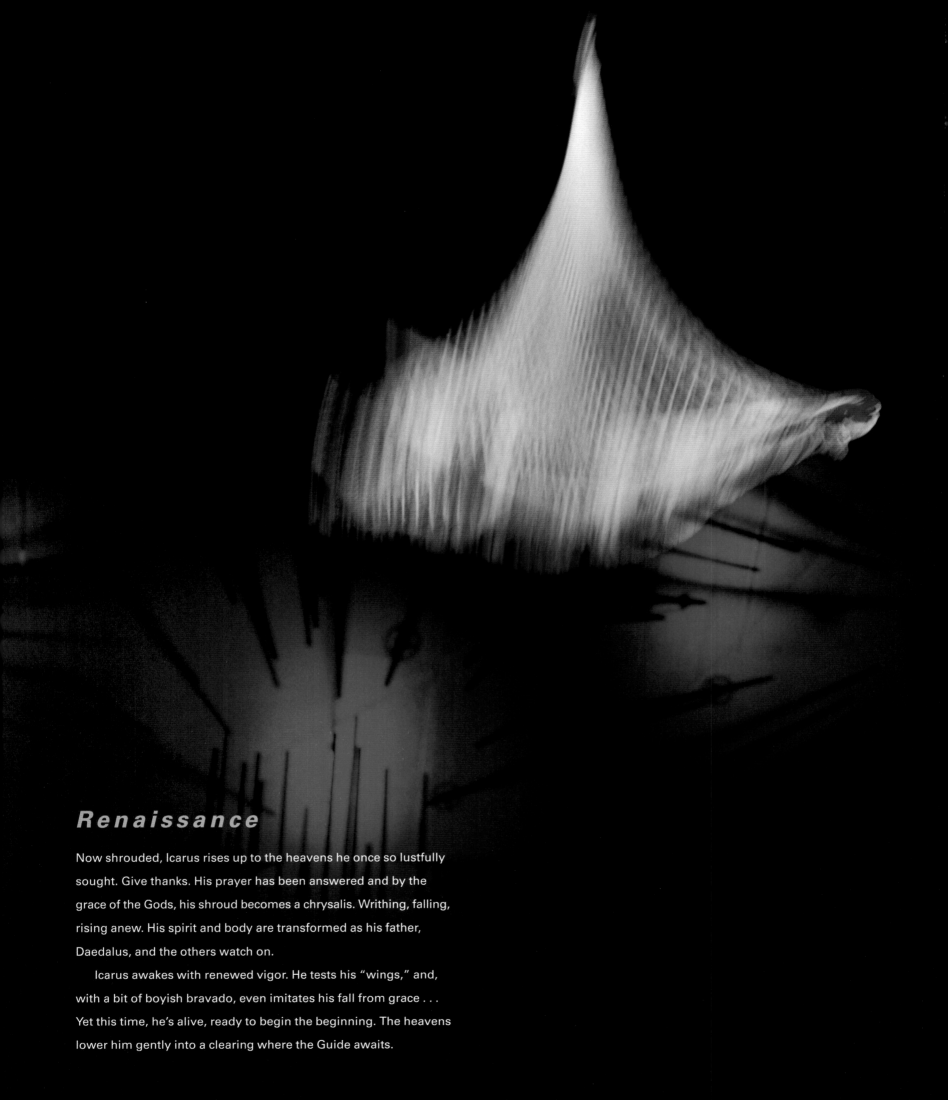

Renaissance

Now shrouded, Icarus rises up to the heavens he once so lustfully
sought. Give thanks. His prayer has been answered and by the
grace of the Gods, his shroud becomes a chrysalis. Writhing, falling,
rising anew. His spirit and body are transformed as his father,
Daedalus, and the others watch on.

    Icarus awakes with renewed vigor. He tests his "wings," and,
with a bit of boyish bravado, even imitates his fall from grace . . .
Yet this time, he's alive, ready to begin the beginning. The heavens
lower him gently into a clearing where the Guide awaits.

Olga

From caterpillar to butterfly. From primeval to promise. Like Icarus,
Olga goes through a metamorphosis of her own. In the first act,
she erupts from a crater in the earth, a volcanic offering. Once on
stage, she twists and turns, a prisoner in her own skin, trying to
free herself from her ill-tailored trappings. Hers is a world of worry,
fear, and fragility. Soon, she'll fall in love with Icarus and her world
will turn, as will ours.

am I

alone to suffer fate again

alone with my immortal pain

or will there be someone to share

my gift

my dance

this breath of air

a second chance at life

but where

am I

Les Amours *first act*

With one wave of his mighty wings, the Guide releases Olga from her subterranean exile. Icarus sees her and is immediately drawn to her side. Their body language is poignant and poetic, yet tentative. Slowly, they draw nearer until finally, their hands embrace.

No sooner have they locked their hands in love, than the heavens revolt. Olga flees underground and Icarus is left desperate, disconsolate as before. The Guide does his best to oppose the malign forces . . . to no avail.

beauty in full blossom

plucked like a common flower

appreciation or jealousy

desire or rage

. . .

with time

all emotions fade

Once again, Icarus and Olga have a chance to clasp hands. And once again, the Gods revolt. Or rather this time, it's the Goddesses who revolt. Are they as jealous of Olga as the Limping Angel is jealous of Icarus? Or are they doing the Limping Angel's dirty work?

The Goddesses descend swiftly and, with the help of some underworld figures, they bind Olga's feet and draw her up into the mouth of heaven. Icarus is left despondent once again, and he's forced to watch as the Goddesses perform their aerial wonders. They're taunting him: *Say good-bye to your love, Icarus. Say good-bye to your dreams of one day reaching the heavens.*

Icarian Games

With the marmot scurrying about in the background, ten Icarians come together to deliver a message of fraternal generosity: we need each other to survive. For Icarus, there's another meaning. If he wants to reach the heavens again, he'll need support . . .

The games reach their finale with two Icarians – perched then launched from the feet of their brothers – simultaneously performing a series of twisting back flips. In the forest as in life, trust is everything.

what's that noise

. . .

    a sign to follow

or a cry from the past

    a glimpse of the future

or a memory held fast

    in the ether

or the other sphere

    but now it's ringing in my ear

oh

what's that noise

The Skywatcher

Part birdman. Part crazed genius. The Skywatcher parades out onto stage with his omnicycle if you will, a fantastic contraption with bells, secret boxes, whistles, and whirligigs designed to capture the sounds and collective souls of the past. He's the master of symphonies, the inveterate inventor. Gangly and disjointed, with feathers akimbo, the Skywatcher also bears comic witness to the love story unfolding between Icarus and Olga.

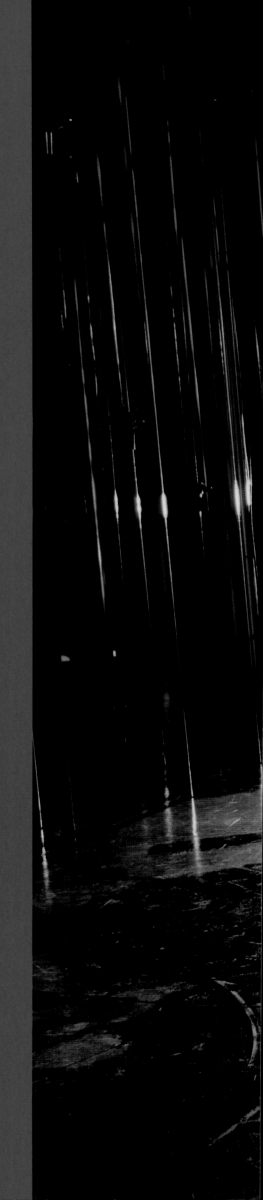

angel of mercy

dove of peace

messenger

of death's release

on a wing and a prayer

you grant new lease

on life

The Guide

Like a mythical creature or a gothic gargoyle, both menace and protector, the Guide is omnipresent: officiating at the sacred circle of the Fall, orchestrating Icarus in his every move. Choreographer and ritual healer. Guardian of time and alchemist of renaissance. The Guide sees all, knows all, controls all.

balls of light

sweep across the sky

like fireflies

waiting to be caught

how long can we imprison them

in our imagination

before they burn out

or fly free

The Gatherers

A moment of poetic repose. Amidst the hostility of the forest, where forces conspire against Icarus and Olga, both in search of self-renewal, the Gatherers come as a pleasant downpour of emotion. A celebration of the elements.

Three young boys receive meteors freshly plucked from the sky. To us, these are celestial bodies, full of power and portent. To the children, they are toys. What follows is a blaze of whirling light, with feats that defy both gravity and imagination. If Icarus was once a falling star, this is surely a symbol of redemption.

Clown Magic

A clear *"mise en abyme"* (narrative layering or duplication): this
act is both a show within a show and a parody of traditional magi-
cians and circus acts. Is it entertainment for the inhabitants of this
strange world? A moment of levity in an otherwise dramatically
charged storyline? Or an opportunity for Cirque du Soleil to poke
lighthearted fun at the weary world of stage?

if not for the clouds

there'd be no air

at least none upon which we could stare

the sun may shine

the winds may blow

rain may fall

and winter snow

but up above

and always near

the clouds hold vast dominion

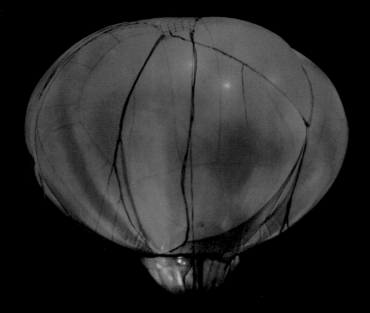

The Cloud

A choir of angelic voices sings solemnly as the Skywatcher appears on stage with a cloud in tow. Shining, pulsating, incandescent blue, the cloud is not well. The Skywatcher lays down the cloud's rope and walks up it, tight, like a stairway to . . . dare we say it? Then, with a sweet paternal kiss on the forehead, he lets the cloud drift off again. Whatever can be done?

In a scene that harkens back to the beginning of our story, the cloud hits the Grand Chapiteau, and suddenly, the light in the cloud is snuffed out. In its place, the cloud coughs up a cacophony of television sounds, suggesting the generations of pollution that have fouled our air.

the holy trinity

three plus three

graces calling

play with me

the heavens await

your destiny

The Goddesses

Six goddesses perched above the audience, suspended within a crystalline cage. Their every movement beckons. Their every gesture, an enticement to Icarus: a promise of what awaits. But he's been burned before.

Triple Trapeze

what the heavens unite

we must tear asunder

wrench the bleeding heart from within

wrest the anxious soul

exorcise the demons

offer them up in sacrifice

your only hope is struggle

The Fire Masters

Icarus now has two reasons to fear the Gods: they took his life once, and now they've taken his love. He must exorcise his fears or resign himself to an existence of pedestrian pursuits.

As the Fire Masters take the stage, the sky opens up, the earth trembles, and the music begins to build. With stomping feet and whirlwind pirouettes, the dancers invoke a storm of arguments defending Icarus. The music comes to a thunderous climax as the Guide looks on, sword in hand.

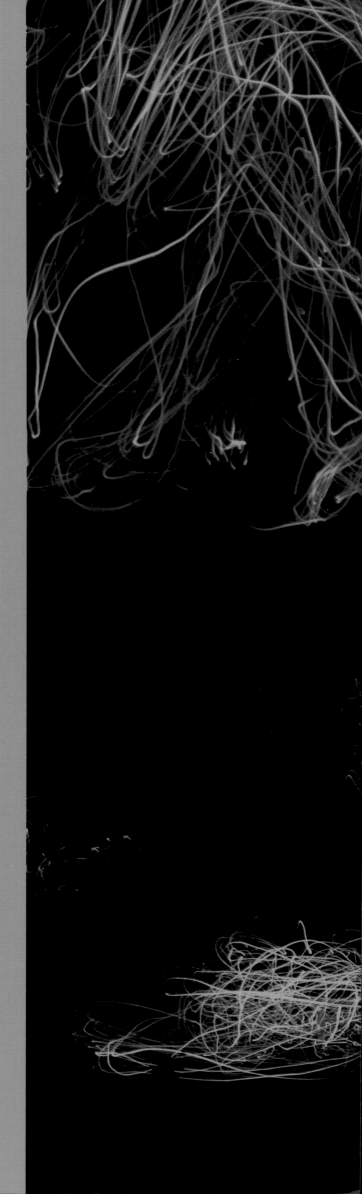

luciole

luz

lumen

light

   all the stars come out tonight

   won't you come and join our flight

   the sky is filled with diamonds

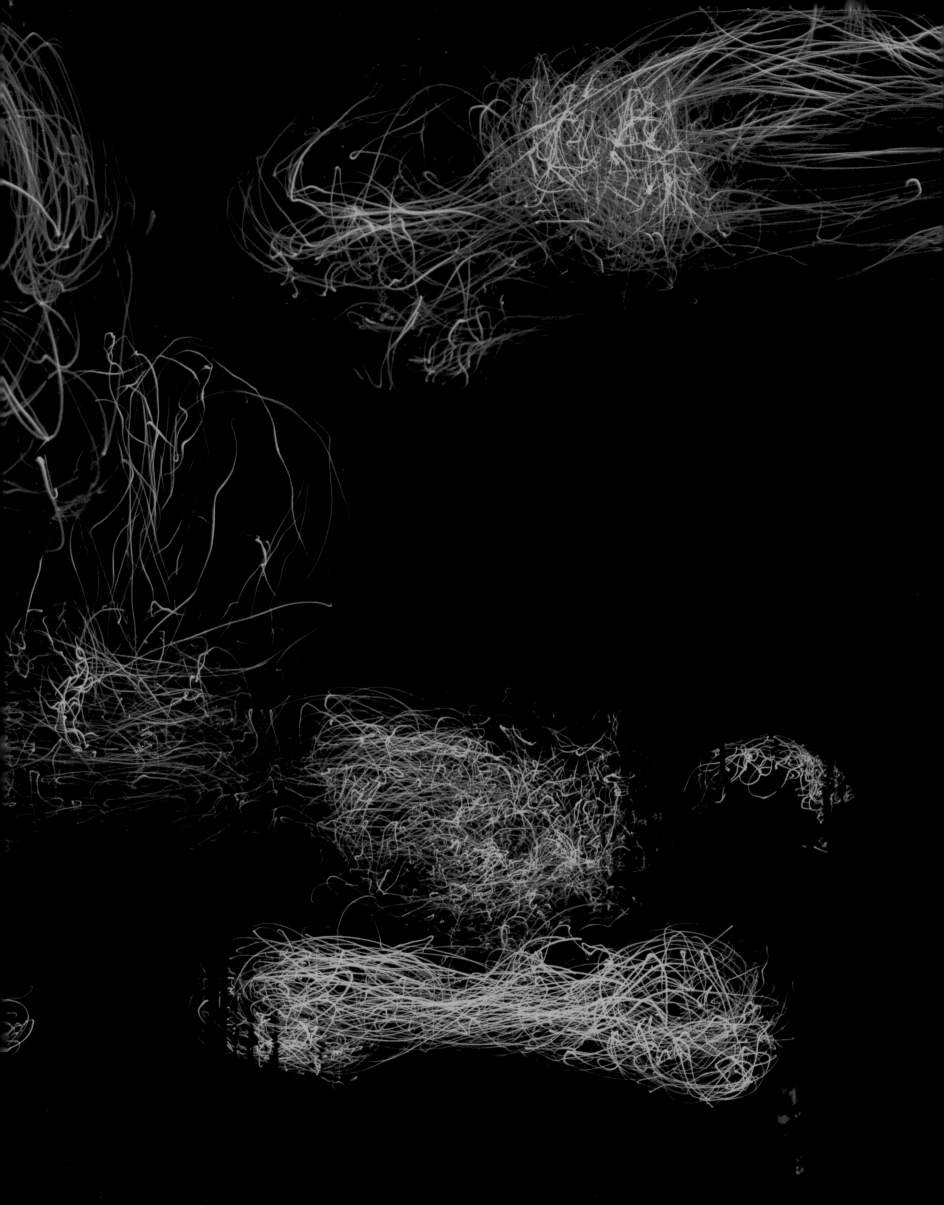

Waltz of the Fireflies

The stage is black. Then slowly, by ones and twos, now dozens and hundreds, the night comes alive with fireflies. Flitting, dancing, hopping, they bring warmth and beauty to the vast emptiness of space.

As gradually as they came, they fade away, leaving a single dancing jewel. As the stage lights come up, we find the Skywatcher, firefly-fishing on the banks of an imaginary river.

from this drop

      all life doth spring

all creatures rise

      all truth doth ring

from this drop

      transparent seed

a force so strong

      desire and need

from this drop

      of tear or rain

the waters

      wash away our pain

the rivers flow to sea

Slippery

Gather round, all creatures aquatic and terrestrial. Couples playfully fish with fowl in the name of love. Anemones, lizards, droplets, and birds dance together in this celebration of the sacred encounter. The stage becomes a river, and for a brief moment the creatures free themselves and become a band of joyous nomads at a tropical carnival.

Claudio's Song

Another change of pace in the storyline. A slim, foreign would-be singer with slicked-back hair does his rendition of the old French classic: *Ne me quitte pas* – Don't leave me. As he sings, the spot-light moves, leaving him in the dark. He hurries frantically, time and time again, trying to remain in the light. To a stage performer, losing the spotlight is tantamount to losing one's life.

hobbled by desires

driven by emotions

they limp through life

supported by a ray of hope

a chance

to get a leg up

The Limping Angels

The Limping Angel and his tribe perform a dance of death. This is their final chance to put the fear of god into Icarus, who seems to be on his last legs, almost unable to go on.

   They try to capture him but the Guide stands guard, his wings beating menacingly. These are the demons who haunt Icarus: the threat of what he might become . . . and the impetus to become something much more.

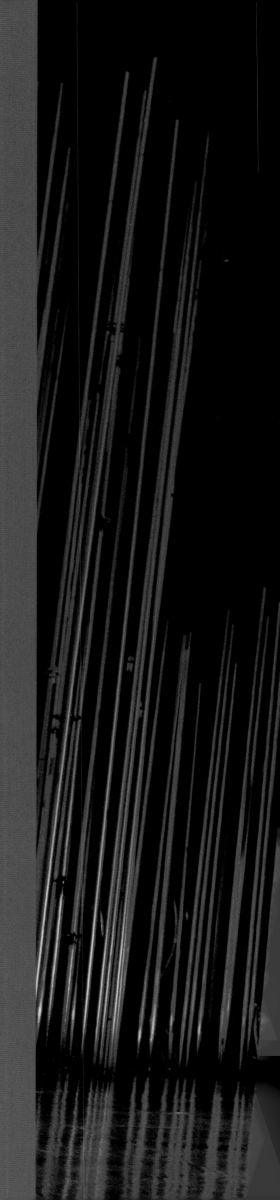

keep your head in the clouds

and one day

you'll see

there's only one way

up

a stairway to the stars

Pas de deux

no night without day

no work without play

no sun without rain

no joy without pain

without you I am less than whole

a demi-being

with half a soul

united we are more than one

we must not be undone

Aerial Straps

In a ballet of perfect symmetry, wrapped in each other's shadow
then flying free, almost bursting the Grand Chapiteau itself,
the twins – Castor and Pollux – perform aerial feats that Icarus
could only dream of. The performance has a message: *all this is
possible, Icarus.* Find the other half of your moon. Become
whole at last. Unite and the heavens will be yours for eternity.

The Juggler

Of course. What better metaphor for the ephemeral quality of
flight? Using ping-pong balls, volleyballs, and pins, the juggler
does his best to defy the law of gravity. But as Icarus knows,
what goes up . . .

where there's a will

there's a way

or at least that's what they say

so pick yourself up

and turn the work into play

flip the problem upside down

find the smile behind the frown

and the night

will turn into day

Lightbulb

The Guide appears on stage with a problem. His light has burned out. Thankfully, the Skywatcher is on hand with a toolbox and an ingenious idea: he strings the Guide up by his feet, spins him counterclockwise, then inserts a new light bulb into his hat. Brilliant.

it's waiting within

    if you'll only let it out

break free your skin

    this is no time for doubt

your future is calling

    there's greatness about

let the transformation begin

Metamorphosis

We had almost forgotten Olga since she was kidnapped by the Goddesses; but not Icarus. He's been dreaming about her since the beginning of time. And now his dreams will come true. Olga comes back to earth, writhing and convulsing like a pupa in her new skin of pure white. She's lowered onto a set of upright canes where she begins an amazing ballet . . . a feat of balance and flexibility and strength. Icarus watches, spellbound by her metamorphosis.

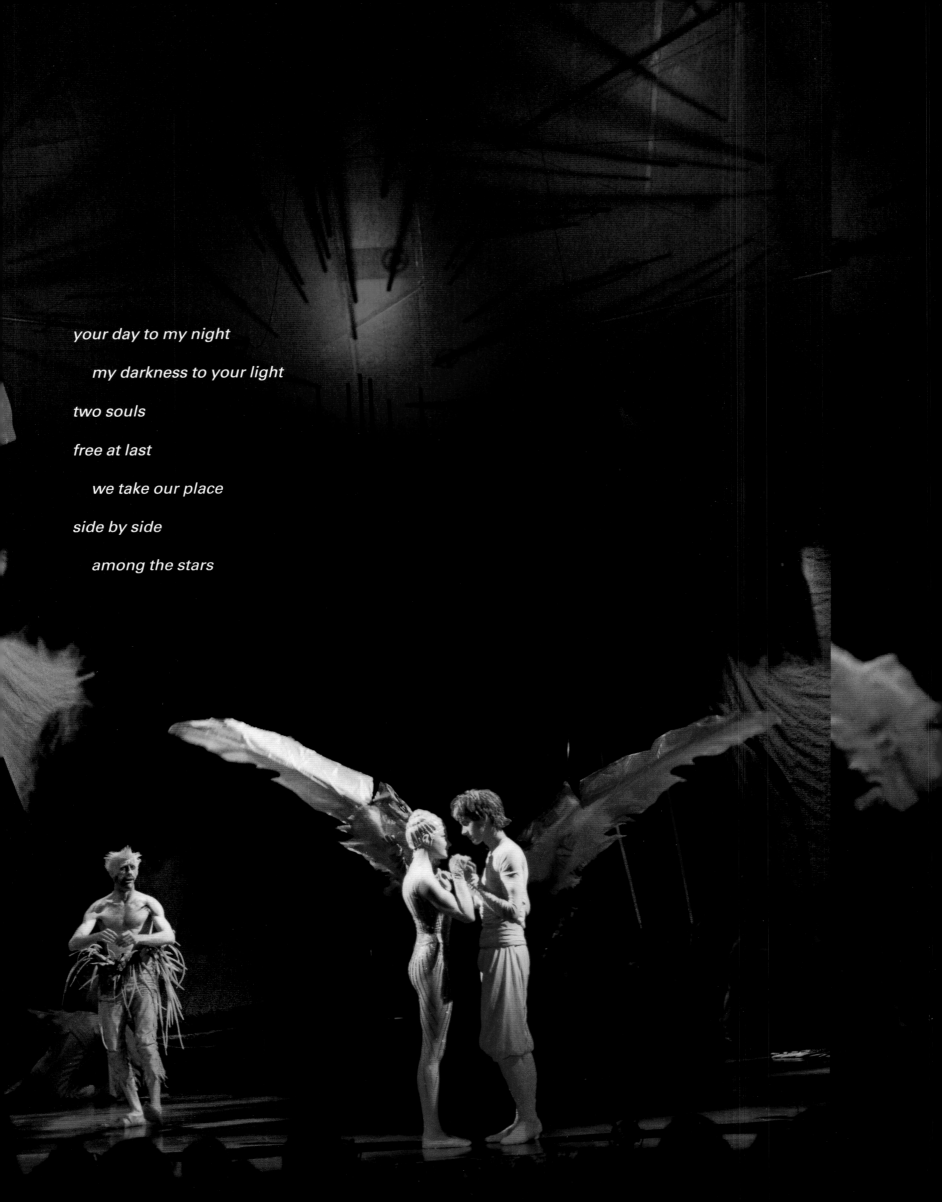

your day to my night

   my darkness to your light

two souls

free at last

   we take our place

side by side

   among the stars

Lovers' Flight

At the end of Olga's metamorphosis, she lays herself before
Icarus. He rises, takes her hand and the two walk side by side to
center stage – a cortege of villagers in tow. The winged Guide
presides over the ceremony as the two rise up into the heavens.

Icarus and Olga consummate their celestial union in a series
of stunningly beautiful aerial maneuvers, then rejoin the crowds
below for what promises to be a breathtaking reception.

if till death do we part

then our life must be art

graceful

sweeping

drawn across the heavens

inspired by nothing less

than love

The Banquet

Like newly crowned royalty, Icarus and Olga take their place at
the table of honor, surrounded by guests and a feast of boundless
bounty. Both have come so far. Both have changed so much.
Everything they sought is now theirs.

Let the celebration begin. One after another, the performers leap
from the Russian swings, soaring effortlessly across the Grand
Chapiteau sky. In the Grand Finale, the acrobats are shot skyward,
performing double, even triple twisting layouts that carry them
gently into the clouds. For Icarus, this is poetry in motion. His
dreams have all come true.

Russian Swings

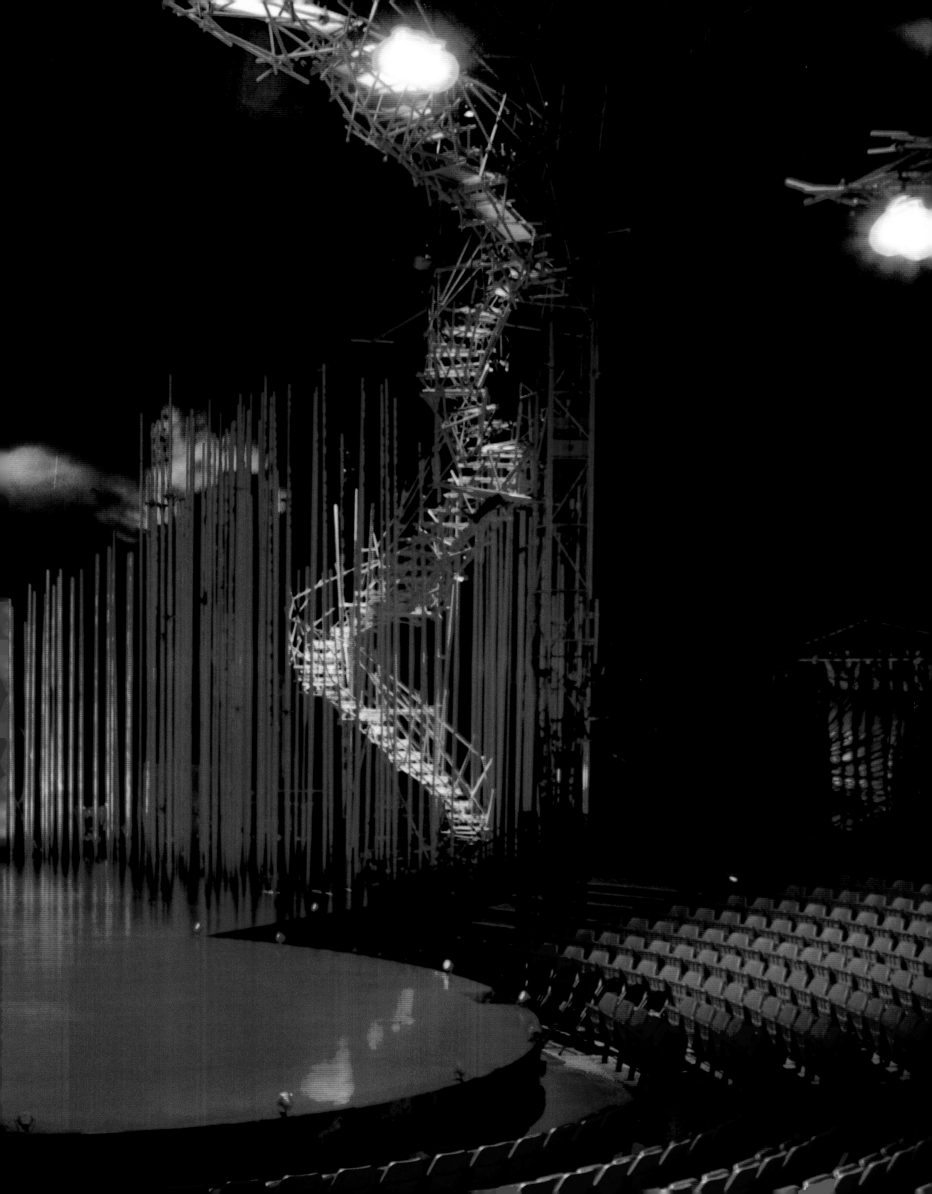

Cirque du Soleil

The journey began in 1982, in Baie-Saint-Paul, Québec, on the northern shores of the
Saint Lawrence River. A group of young street artists organized an impromptu show
for the community. Driven by the delight of their audience, the performers started an
entertainers' festival. From the smallest seed grows the tallest tree.

Cirque du Soleil was created in 1984, from a truly unique concept: a striking and
dramatic mix of circus arts and street entertainment with fantastic costumes, artistic
lighting, original music, breathtaking acrobatics… and not a single animal.

Today, Cirque du Soleil has several shows touring the planet and others featured on
permanent stages in resorts and hotels. They have captured the hearts of millions of
people the world over. Wherever the wind carries the Cirque, they will always be home.

The Making of an Angel

For Guy Laliberté, co-founder of Cirque du Soleil, the creation of a production is a labor of love. "It's like a new baby: you have to clean it and pamper it and teach it to walk so that one day it can walk on its own. The dream is always about bringing a new baby to life." And, as with every new Cirque du Soleil production, the creation of *Varekai* took months of passionate struggle and commitment in the face of often overwhelming technical and physical challenges. "It's not a formula that you repeat over and over," says Laliberté, "It's a challenge and if we fail, it's OK, because we know that we gave it everything we had to give." Eighteen years and thirteen productions later, the dream is very much a reality and the success of Cirque du Soleil is known the world over.

One of the Cirque's longtime dream-weavers is Andrew Watson. "Guy came to me in London and asked if I wanted to change my life completely." Being a creator, he jumped at the chance and was named Director of Creation. Early in the process, Watson contacted Montréal stage director, Dominic Champagne, who immediately answered the call. "It was like a gift that fell from the sky. But I told Guy, 'This is a risk you're taking. I've never done anything like this before. If you're willing to share the risk with me, let's go."

In September of 2001, the creative team and all the main performers came together for the first time. Georgian dancers, circus artists from Moscow, a choreographer with crutches and skateboards from New York . . . Dominic Champagne remembers the cultural clashes and the energy in the room with a sparkle in his eye. "You have no idea what's going to happen but you know it's going to be something very big."

One of the first major decisions that Dominic Champagne made was to give *Varekai* a more prominent narrative structure than in other Cirque du Soleil productions. The premise was simple: what if Icarus had fallen into a forest inhabited by a community of artists and survivors? *Varekai* begins with such a fall and follows Icarus as he struggles to rise anew. In the director's words "*Varekai* is a tribute to the art of living, of being together, of people surviving with their art."

Risk, danger, and the struggle to rise above and meet any challenge, no matter how great: these are the forces that drive the creative spirit. They are also powerful themes in *Varekai*. And the parallel between the evolution of the production and that of its two main characters – Icarus and Olga – is nothing short of striking. All exist in a world where anything is possible. For, as Dominic Champagne believes, "When you believe that anything is possible, you allow yourself to dream things that you would otherwise never dream of."

Slowly but certainly *Varekai* began to take form. Internationally acclaimed Japanese costume designer, Eiko Ishioka was invited to join the team. She brought with her a profound sense of natural beauty and otherworldly imagination to the characters. Set designer Stéphane Roy created a sparse, metaphorical forest. "I have to give the artists the feeling of going somewhere. The forest is the context of life, experimentation, and fear. The forest is magic and the audience must feel that anything can happen here." Composer Violaine Corradi began scoring the production almost as though it were a film. "My work as a composer is to communicate the story to the audience. My mandate as a creator is to remind people about the beauty on earth."

As with life itself, creative endeavors are subject to radical change without notice. Late in the process, Guy Laliberté told the team he was unhappy with one of the main acts. In his view, it simply didn't work. He asked Dominic to go back to the drawing board. The team was stunned, almost heartbroken. Opening night lay looming in the distance and they had to rethink an entire act. Narrative. Choreography. Costumes. Music. Champagne remembers the moment: "if there's no risk of failing, it's not a risk . . . thankfully, chaos is a creative force." The team pulled together. The spirit of community and the level of commitment were amazing. The working philosophy was clear: you hit a hard patch and you go around it. You keep on going, you keep on believing.

Seven weeks from opening night the cast and crew visited the Grand Chapiteau for the very first time. There was a keen sense of awe. Andrew Watson: "this is our cathedral, this is honestly a very moving moment for me." For the next two, three, perhaps five years, this will be their home. It's not just a new production, everything was new: dressing rooms, kitchen, trailers, exercise and stretching areas. And it can all be packed up and shipped to a new city in a matter of days.

For the next few weeks, the creative team and the performers struggled to see their vision through, to take their place on the stage. Every act, every costume, every movement had to come together seamlessly. Thousands of hours of intense training and rehearsals had to blend perfectly. There was more than pride at stake. All of the aerial maneuvers are performed without safety nets or wires and the possibility of death or serious injury is always a reality. Rigging Director, Jacque Paquin is responsible for the lives of the performers. But like the creators, he would not allow himself to be driven by fear: "I cannot fear what I'm doing because I'm asking the artists and acrobats to risk their own lives in performing their art. There can be no fear. Stress and anxiety yes, but no fear."

With opening night only a few weeks away, the fatigue was beginning to show. Tensions were mounting. Everyone had their own needs and every performer was fighting to bring their art to life. Like Guy Laliberté, Violaine Corradi compared the process to that of giving birth. "This last phase is like labor. Everyone's pushing, pushing together." Dominic Champagne was ready to set his baby free. "It's time for us to step back and let Varekai take its place in the world . . . it doesn't belong to us anymore." The Premiere performance – April 24, 2002, Montreal. The crowd gathered: paparazzi, politicians, stage and theatre critics, and celebrities from afar. This was a tough audience. Dominic Champagne gave his team one final word of encouragement. "The audience is here for you. Give them your souls. Touch their hearts. There are only three things that count out there: emotion, emotion, emotion." The lights came up and Varekai came to life amidst a deafening roar of delight. Backstage, performers watched on video as their fellow artists performed flawlessly. As the performers came off the stage, they were greeted with an explosion of joy and an outpouring of emotions.

After what seemed like an interminable standing ovation, the team came together to salute their director, Dominic Champagne. Laughter and tears flowed freely as months of tireless commitment and energy finally came to fruition. Guy Laliberté was beside himself with pride and excitement. A performer himself, he bowed humbly in a gesture of gratitude to the countless people who helped make his dreams come true. *This is for you.* Varekai *is yours forever.*

Home is where the heart is . . .

"Wherever the wind carries us, we'll always be home." It's a powerful nomadic theme, one that is certainly not lost on the cast and crew. After all, *Varekai* is a traveling show, with nearly twenty North American cities scheduled in the first two years alone. It's a given that they'll feel right at home wherever they go because they take their home with them.

Moving from city to city is a logistical feat that rivals the artistic feats for which the Cirque du Soleil is so well known. It takes seven days and literally hundreds of people to set up the entire site – from the Grand Chapiteau, right down to the kitchen, the school and the exercise equipment – and every member of the cast and crew is involved to some degree.

If the Grand Chapiteau is home, the cast and crew are one big extended family. Often thousands of miles away from their native lands, the performers form close ties to their colleagues, sharing everything from meals to rooms. Indeed, the very nature of their art encourages tightly-knit relationships: understanding, trust, and an almost uncanny sense of the other are of paramount importance to acrobats and aerial artists. Your partner is quite literally your link to life.

And what a life it is, Anton Chelnokov got his first taste of circus life in 1990 as a young boy, when he toured with the Cirque du Soleil production *Saltimbanco*. When the tour was over, he returned to his native Moscow, but ironically, never felt quite settled. He dreamed of the day he could join his second family on the road once again . . . and his dream came true. Today, Anton plays the role of Icarus in *Varekai* and it's easy to see that the Grand Chapiteau is where he really feels at home.

The Creators

Guy Laliberté: *Creative Guide*

Dominic Champagne: *Writer and Director*

Andrew Watson: *Director of Creation*

Stéphane Roy: *Set Designer*

Eiko Ishioka: *Costume Designer*

Violaine Corradi: *Composer and Musical Director*

Michael Montanaro: *Choreographer*

Bill Shannon: *Choreographer*

Jaque Paquin: *Rigging Designer*

Nol Van Genuchten: *Lighting Designer*

François Bergeron: *Sound Designer*

Francis Laporte: *Projection Designer*

Dominic Champagne, Writer and Director

"*I think artists have the responsibility to ask questions about the world around them and to celebrate new worlds. All of my plays are about trying to achieve one's dream.*" A multitalented and prolific artist, Dominic Champagne has been a forceful presence on the Quebec cultural scene since leaving the National Theatre School of Canada in 1987. His more than one hundred accomplishments for the stage and television have earned him a host of awards and honors.

Directing Varekai marks Champagne's first collaboration with Cirque du Soleil, but also signifies a return to his roots. At the age of twenty, penniless and alone in Greece, he joined the circus! What did the experience teach him? "*The circus is a place where fraternity is possible and where the clashing of cultures is an exceptional source of creativity. The multiethnic environment at Cirque du Soleil is inspiring. It feeds my creative universe.*" The grandson of a judge and a welder, Champagne strives to reach both his grandfathers in every project he does.

Andrew Watson, Director of Creation

"*My role is to create synergy between the members of the creative team and to facilitate their work. Since this is our first time working together, this show's signature is necessarily different than that of previous Cirque du Soleil productions. The risk is deliberate. Indeed, the distinguishing feature of this artistic company is its willingness to take risks.*"

Andrew Watson joined the London-based Gerry Cottle Circus at the age of twenty-four and later worked for the German circus troupe Roncalli. In 1987 he joined the team of *We Reinvent the Circus,* the show that was to be the Cirque du Soleil's first major North American tour. Throughout his career as a Cirque du Soleil acrobat, Watson won several honors and awards, including the Clown d'argent at the Festival International du Cirque de Monte-Carlo in 1990. He left the ring that year and subsequently held positions of director of casting and artistic training, artistic coordinator, and artistic director for the Cirque du Soleil. From 1994 to 1999, he was mainly involved in the shows *Saltimbanco, Alegría,* and *Quidam.* He then left Cirque and returned to London to join the New Millenium Experience Company, developing aerial acts and training acrobatic artists for the *New Millenium Dome Central Show.* After the year-2000 festivities were accomplished, Watson returned to Montréal to oversee the creation of *Varekai,* marking a new stage in his artistic career.